D1351632

REMEMBER THE SEVENTIES

A pictorial history of a stirring decade

REMEMBER THE SEVENTIES

A pictorial history of a stirring decade

Bath • New York • Singapore • Hong Kong • Cologne • Delhi
Melbourne • Amsterdam • Johannesburg • Auckland • Shenzhen

This edition published by Parragon in 2011
Parragon
Queen Street House
4 Queen Street
Bath, BA1 1HE

www.parragon.com

Created and produced by:
Endeavour London Ltd.
21-31 Woodfield Road
London W9 2BA

With great thanks to the team at Endeavour London Ltd. – Jennifer Jeffrey, Kate Pink, Franziska Payer-Crockett and Liz Ihre

Text © Parragon Books Ltd 2007

ISBN 978-1-4454-4694-3

Printed in China

All images courtesy of Getty Images who is grateful to the following photographers and image libraries represented by Getty Images for their kind assistance.

20th Century Fox: 24-25, 44, 183; ABC: 73; Agence France Presse: 18, 31, 60, 67(b), 75, 84-86, 90-91, 94(t), 99, 108, 123-125, 130-134, 142-143, 158, 160, 161(b), 165, 175, 197(b), 198-199, 207-208(t), 217, 222, 226(t), 227-228, 235, 241-242, 246-247; Allied Artists: 98; Cinema Center Films: 26(b); Columbia Pictures: 205; Liaison/Dirck Halstead: 56; NASA: 28-29, 80-83, 141; Paramount : 26(t), 126-127, 202; Roger Viollet: 135, 162, 212-213; Tim Graham Photo Library: 193; Time & Life Pictures: 10(t), 12, 14-15, 28, 38-39, 45, 54-55, 61, 65, 73, 78, 80, 82-83, 88, 101, 103-105, 141, 170, 178, 196-197(t), 200, 204, 218-219, 223, 226(b), 230-233, 253-254; United Artists: 72, 182, 203; Universal Pictures: 99

Cover images clockwise from left to right:
John Travolta on the set of *Saturday Night Fever*, 1977.
© Getty Images

Surface of Mars taken from Viking I, the first colour images from another planet, 1976. © Time & Life Pictures/Getty Images

Nadia Comaneci wins three golds at the Summer Olympic Games in Montreal, 1976. © Getty Images

Pope John Paul II's first public appearance after his election to the papacy, 1978. © Time & Life Pictures/Getty Images

President Gerald Ford reviewing Chinese troops with Chinese Premier Deng Xiaoping, 1976. © Getty Images

The Sex Pistols performing live onstage during their final tour, 1978. © Getty Images

View of lower Manhattan skyline with World Trade Center Towers and Statue of Liberty, 1973. © Time & Life Pictures/Getty Images

Freddie Mercury lead singer of rock quartet Queen on stage, 1977.
© Getty Images

Middle image:
Queen Elizabeth II with Princess Anne, Earl Mountbatten and the Duke of Edinburgh on the balcony of Buckingham Palace during her Silver Jubilee, 1977.
© Getty Images

Frontispiece
David Bowie performs as his alter ego Ziggy Stardust in 1973.

Page 7
"...Implacable in hate, resolved to ruin or to rule the state..." At the height of the civil war, two men fight on in what is left of President Franjieh's palace in Beirut, Lebanon, 26 March 1976.

Book Contents

DVD Contents

Introduction

Some eras gain an identity all their own. The Swinging Sixties, equally memorable for political reasons, has gone down in history as pre-eminently a time of sexual liberation and daring fashion. Other eras have a label thrust upon them by circumstances that preceded their control. The Thirties were Hungry not through any fault of their own, but because of the sins and omissions of earlier wars and economic crises. And some eras have no clear identity. The Seventies were essentially years during which the energy of the 1960s ran out, and millions of dreamers came back to earth with a bump.

War ended in Vietnam, broke out repeatedly in the Middle East, carved out the new state of Bangladesh, tore Lebanon apart, and shattered the hopes of Biafra. New regimes took over in Greece, Argentina, and Chile. Franco's rule came to an end in Spain. The Ayatollah Khomeini was expelled from Iran in 1978, to return a year later when the Shah was forced to flee. Fighting intensified in Rhodesia, which failed to survive the decade, becoming Zimbabwe in 1979. Soviet troops warily entered Afghanistan. Almost all these events sowed the seeds of immense future misery.

Terrorists, and there were plenty of them, became celebrities. Baader-Meinhof, Leila Khaled, Patty Hearst, the Red Brigades all had their following of mixed-up fans. Law enforcement responded to real or perceived threats, and violent death came to streets and campuses in the most developed societies on the planet. The growling of discontent was heard in the shipyards of Gdansk, in Bogside and Derry, in the dust of Soweto, and on the trading post at Wounded Knee. CS gas and rubber bullets made their public debuts.

In the midst of death, there was more death. Musically, Hendrix, Joplin, and Presley sang their last, their bodies finally submitting to prolonged abuse. But the show went on, with new superstars replacing the old – Bowie, Springsteen, Led Zeppelin, the Bee Gees, and the Osmonds. The movie industry found gold in a series of blockbusters and shock-horror films, among them *The Godfather I* and *II*, *The Omen*, *Jaws*, *Star Wars*, and *The Exorcist*.

And the People's Republic of China at last made its formal entry into the United Nations.

Despite good *karma* and great *gurus*, **The Beatles** went their separate long and winding roads in 1970. Yoko Ono was blamed by devoted fans and pop purists. (*Left*) Paul and Linda McCartney dig the peat and breathe the good clean air of the Mull of Kintyre, January 1970. (*Right*) John Lennon carries Yoko through the snow on North Jutland.

Architects of Black Power in the 1970s. (*Above*) **David Hilliard** strides ahead of Jean Genet (extreme left) past national guardsmen at a student rally at Yale University, May 1970. (*Right*) **Angela Davis**, Assistant Professor of Philosophy at the University of California, is arrested on murder and kidnap charges, New York, October 1970. (*Far right*) Black Panther member Angela Davis, August 1970.

🅒 **track 1**

Thirteen months after their protest at the Democrat Convention of 1968, the Chicago Eight came to trial. (*Left*) **Abbie Hoffman** at a Black Panther Rally, May 1970; (*right*) **Jerry Rubin**, with Peter Fonda looking on, at a Senators for Peace Rally, Madison Square Garden, March 1970.

On 4 May 1970 students gathered at **Kent State University**, Ohio to protest at the escalation of the Vietnam War and the US incursion into Cambodia. National guardsmen (*above*) were called in. The students hurled stones at them.

The national guard opened fire. (*Above*) Mary Ann Vecchio kneels over the body of **Jeffrey Glenn Miller**, one of four students killed. Speaking of campus unrest, Ronald Reagan said: "If it takes a bloodbath, let's get it over with."

The August Bank Holiday **Pop Festival** on Britain's Isle of Wight ran at a loss, as many of the 600,000 who attended gate-crashed the proceedings. (*Left and above*) Crowds gather at East Afton Farm. (*Right*) **Jimi Hendrix** at his last gig – he died a month later.

🔘 **track 2**

In September 1970, the **PLO** blew up four planes they had hijacked, demanding the release of many of their members. (*Above*) One of the planes, a VC-10, destroyed in Amman. (*Left*) **Leila Khaled**, who made an unsuccessful attempt to hijack a fifth plane.

When news broke of the **death of Charles de Gaulle** on 10 November 1970 (*left*), Georges Pompidou announced: "France is widowed". Over 40,000 came to the General's funeral in his home town of Colombey-les-Deux-Eglises, Haute-Marne (*right*), paying their respects to the man who had habitually cast himself in the role of saviour of his country.

By 1970, when the mini-skirt had gone as high as it could go, the fashion houses decided it was time for **the Maxi**. (*Left*) Dior's black and white wool coats and snakeskin hats, London, March 1970. (*Right*) **Shirley Bassey**, in white mink hat and coat, and Aston Martin DBS, 6 November 1970.

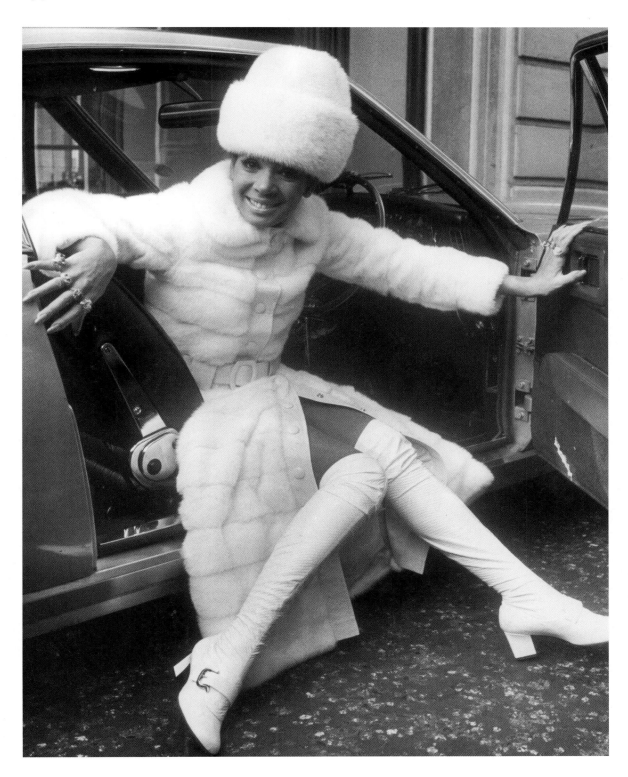

Of the films of 1970, **Myra Breckinridge**, starring Raquel Welch (*left*), attempted to shock but only disappointed – "About as funny as a child molester," said *Time*. **Patton: Lust for Glory**, however, gained Oscars for Best Picture, Writer and Director, as well as for George C Scott (*above*) as Best Male Actor.

Among other films, Steve McQueen's convincing Grand Prix driving carried **Le Mans** (*far right*); mawkish romance and the line "Love means never having to say you're sorry..." carried **Love Story**, with Ali MacGraw and Ryan O'Neal (*above*); and massacre, messages, and mordancy carried **Little Big Man**, with Dustin Hoffman (*right*).

Two years after the first steps on the Moon came the first drive on the Moon. Astronauts on the **Apollo 15** mission (*far left*) covered 13 square kilometres (5 square miles) in their Lunar Roving Vehicle. (*Above*) Commander David Scott returns with rock samples, 28 August 1971. (*Left*) James Irwin in front of the lunar module *Falcon*.

In the autumn of 1971 Emperor **Hirohito** became the first ruler of Japan to leave the country in 2,000 years. His visit to seven Western countries was an act of atonement for the events of 1941. (*Above*) Hirohito and Queen Elizabeth II enter Buckingham Palace, 4 October.

General **Idi Amin Dada** seized power in Uganda in January 1971, while the country's former ruler, Milton Obote was out of the country. (*Above*) In the opulent surroundings of the Elysée Palace, Amin (left) pays an official visit on President Pompidou, 16 September 1971.

The **IRA** extended its campaign of terrorist attacks in the 1970s. One of its targets was the Post Office Tower in Tottenham Court Road – the tallest building in London. (*Above*) The gaping hole left by the bomb, 31 October. (*Right*) Damage to the revolving restaurant is inspected – the restaurant was never reopened to the public.

The partition of the Indian sub-continent in 1947 had been hastily executed.
By the early 1970s, the drive to create the independent state of **Bangladesh** out
of East Pakistan had gathered violent momentum. (*Above*) Indian Mukti Bahini
guerrilla troops prepare to execute men who collaborated with the Pakistani Army.
(*Right*) The bodies of three local traitors lie on the lines at Jhihargachi station.

In 1971 **Andy Warhol** opened a video factory, staged a play, painted portraits, and attended the German premiere of his film *Trash*: (*left*) with stars of the film Joe Dallesandro and Jane Forth. (*Above*) Warhol's *The Most Wanted Men* exhibition at the Tate Gallery, London, February 1971.

(*Above*) Broadway sublimity, with Jeff Fenholt as the eponymous **Jesus Christ Superstar**, October 1971. (*Right*) The Temple of Spectacle: staff parade for the opening of **Disney World** in Orlando, Florida.

🔘 **track 4**

Contrasting fashions. (*Left*) Conservative
Party candidate John Milman with a dozen
supporters in their **Hot Pants**. (*Above*) Lesley
Hornby, better known as Twiggy, models the
Oxford Bags that she wore in the Ken Russell
film *The Boy Friend*, 26 April 1971.

The tiger comes to town... (*Above*) The fibre-glass doorway to the **Tyger Tyger** boutique in Kensington Church Street, London, 2 September 1971. (*Right*) A young **tiger cub** and Air Stewardess promote the new uniform for National Airlines, 16 March 1971.

Law enforcement the tough way… (*Left*) Gene Hackman as Popeye Doyle in William Friedkin's **The French Connection**. (*Right*) Clint Eastwood as Harry Callahan in Don Siegel's **Dirty Harry**. The success of the two films led to a spate of "dirty" cop movies.

The British Army had initially been welcomed as saviours by Catholics in Northern Ireland. By 1971 goodwill on both sides was severely tested. In February the first British soldier was killed. A further 41 died before the year ended and another 64 in 1972. Faced with an escalation of violence, the Northern Ireland Prime Minister Brian Faulkner persuaded the British Government to introduce a policy of internment without trial, using powers dating back to the 1920s and the Old Troubles. On 9 August 300 people were detained. And riots broke out in Republican areas of Belfast, Derry, and Newry. The killing continued. On 7 September civilian deaths during these new "Troubles" reached one hundred. And then came Bloody Sunday.

(*Left*) **British troops in Belfast, three days after internment without trial was introduced. (***Above***) A dead RUC officer, slumped at the wheel of his bullet-ridden car, 16 October 1971.**

Life goes on... (*Above*) A member of the Scots Greys, Belfast, 20 April 1971. (*Right*) Eight months later, a gang of children in cheekier mood light fires and jeer at soldiers and reporters, 7 December. (*Below*) An armoured car takes a British soldier and his Catholic bride to their wedding reception, 3 December 1971.

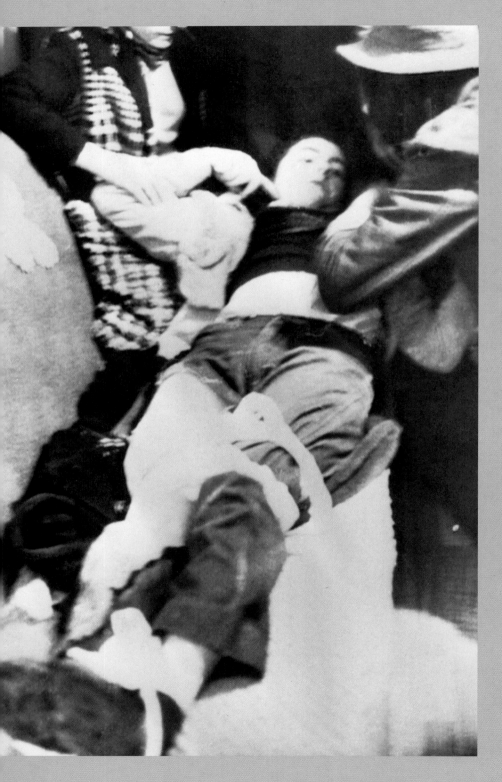

A victim of the Bloody Sunday massacre, Derry, 30 January 1972. British paratroopers killed 13 civilians and wounded others during a civil rights march.

Bloody Sunday presented the Republican cause with a great propaganda victory. (*Left*) Members of the Parachute Regiment threaten civil rights demonstrators during the violence of that day. (*Above*) Relatives of those killed in the massacre at the funeral of some of the victims, 8 February 1972.

The Cunard flagship liner **Queen Elizabeth** was launched in 1938 and spent much of World War II as a troopship. After 25 years as a cruise ship and transatlantic liner, the ship became a floating university in Hong Kong harbour in 1969. (*Left*) The *Queen Elizabeth* is destroyed by fire, Hong Kong, 9 January 1972.

In February 1972, US President Nixon spent a week in **China**, where he spent 15 hours discussing Taiwan, Korea, and other problems with Prime Minister Zhou Enlai. (*Above*, left to right) Zhou Enlai, an interpreter, Mao Zedong, Nixon, and adviser Henry Kissinger. (*Left*) Off duty, the President and Pat Nixon visit the Great Wall. (*Right*) At a banquet, Nixon gazes speculatively at what his chopsticks have picked up.

In May 1972 Nixon was in Moscow, where he and the Soviet leader Leonid Brezhnev signed the **SALT Treaty**, limiting nuclear missile systems in both countries. (*Right*) Brezhnev (right, seated) and Dr Henry Kissinger (standing second from left) look on while Nixon (left) signs the Treaty. The two leaders agreed to do their utmost to avoid "military confrontations".

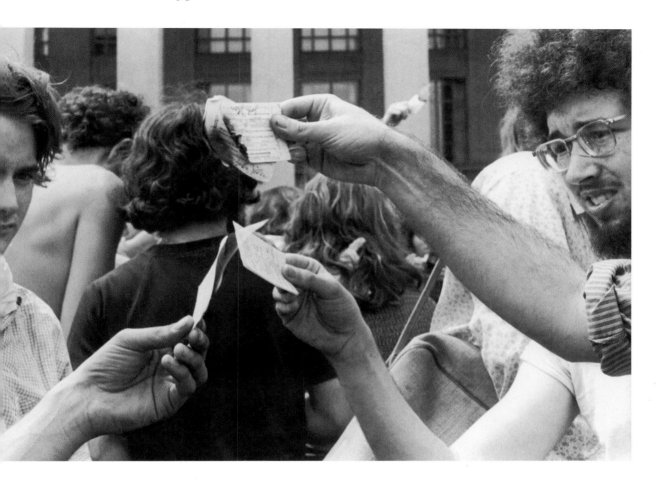

Although there was talk of peace at international levels, the war in Vietnam continued, and opposition to it mounted. (*Right*) Some of the 30,000 demonstrators against the war on parade in New York, 27 April 1972. (*Above*) **Antiwar protesters** burn their draft cards at the Pentagon, 22 May. (*Left*) Police break up a demonstration at the Capitol, Washington DC, 25 May.

The killing and maiming continued.
(*Right*) A **South Vietnamese farmer**
and his baby, wounded by North
Vietnamese artillery fire in Quang Tri
province, April 1972. (*Above*) "Hanoi
Jane", the US film star and anti-war
activist **Jane Fonda**, talks with North
Vietnam's Deputy Prime Minister
Nguyen Duy Trinh, Hanoi, 21 July 1972.

An unlikely headline hitter in 1972 was the Final of the **World Chess Championship**, fought with Cold War intensity between Boris Spassky of the USSR (left) and Bobby Fischer of the USA. (*Above*) Fischer, the eventual winner, arrives for his third match at the Exhibition Hall, Reykjavík, Iceland, 17 July 1972.

Stars of the **1972 Olympic Games** in Munich were Mark Spitz (*above*) who swam his way to seven gold medals, three of them in relays, the other four individual medals in 100 Metres and 200 Metres freestyle, and 100 Metres and 200 Metres butterfly; and Lasse Viren of Finland (*right*), who won gold in the 5,000 Metres and 10,000 Metres, breaking Olympic and World records. The darling of the Games was Soviet gymnast Olga Korbut (*far right*), who won three gold medals.

On 4 September, terrorists from the **Black September** Organisation (BSO) killed two Israeli athletes and took another nine Israelis as hostages, all of whom were later killed in a chaotic shoot-out at Munich Airport. (*Above*) A German official attempts to negotiate with one of the BSO. (*Right*) members of the Israeli Olympic team leave Munich, 7 September. (*Left*) Israeli citizens weep as the dead are brought home.

The tyranny of **General Idi Amin Dada** (*right*) hit his Ugandan Asian subjects in 1972. They were expelled from the country *en masse*. (*Above*) Some of the 30,000 refugees who fled to England arrive at Stansted Airport, 18 September 1972.

Top hats for top pop stars.
(*Far left*) **Alice Cooper**, whose
School's Out was a big hit in 1972.
(*Above*) Glam Rock **T Rex** stars
Mickey Finn (on left) and Marc
Bolan at the time of their album
Electric Warrior and the single
Metal Guru. (*Left*) Noddy Holder,
lead singer with **Slade**, at Wembley
Stadium, 30 October 1972.

Decadence in Paris and Berlin... (*Left*) Bernardo Bertolucci (on right) directs Marlon Brando and Maria Schneider on the set of the 1972 film **Last Tango in Paris**. (*Right*) Liza Minnelli, as Sally Bowles, belts out one of the Kander and Ebb numbers from Bob Fosse's **Cabaret**.

After a million and a quarter deaths, combatants in the war met to discuss a **Vietnam Peace Agreement**. The talks took place at the Hotel Majestic in Paris, around an enormous table (*left*) which symbolized the gulf that existed between North and South Vietnamese. (*Above*) Le Duc Tho, North Vietnam's chief negotiator, waves to Dr Henry Kissinger after the signing of the ceasefire, January 1973.

After 15 years in exile, **General Juan Perón** returned to Argentina
in June 1973, to be greeted by 3.5 million people. The recently
elected President, Dr Hector Campora, stepped down, and Perón
was triumphantly re-elected. (*Above*) Perón (left) and Campora
embrace at Fiumicino Airport, Rome, 27 March 1973. (*Right*)
Perón's second wife, Isabelita, Vice-President of Argentina.

At the time of completion, late in 1973, the twin towers of the **World Trade Center** (on right of picture) were together the tallest buildings in the world. Designed by Minoru Yamasaki, they stood 110 storeys high, comprised almost 4 per cent of Manhattan's total office space, and cost $750 million to build. A year later they were topped by the Sears Tower in Chicago.

Skylab 1 was launched on 14 May 1973.
It weighed 75 tonnes and was America's first
space station. Damaged during its launch,
Skylab required attention by its first crew.
(*Above*) A photo in space showing broken
cables on main body, all that remained of a
missing wing. (*Right*) Dr Owen K Garriott during
his record-breaking seven hour spacewalk.

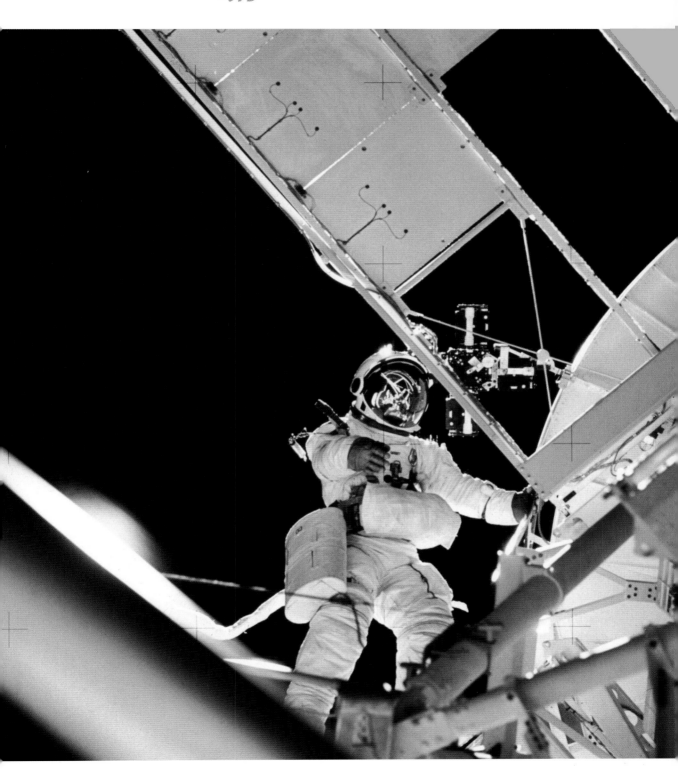

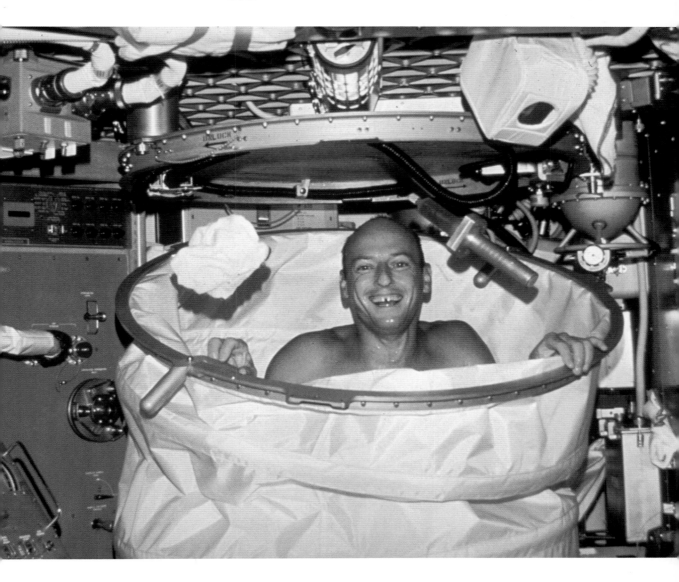

🔘 **track 11**

Three crews visited Skylab during 1973, in May, July, and November. Two of the original crew work and relax: (*left*) Astronaut Joe Kerwin floats in **zero gravity**. (*Above*) Charles "Pete" Conrad with weightless sponge in the collapsible shower stall on board Skylab. During the 28-day first mission, many experiments were conducted into the astronaut's adaptability to micro-gravity.

Unhappy alliance. (*Left*) General **Augusto Pinochet** (left) and Chilean President **Salvador Allende** face the press after Allende had appointed Pinochet head of the army, 23 August 1973. (*Above*) Three weeks later, Pinochet's men fire down on La Moneda Palace, Santiago, as the army stages a coup. Allende was killed and Pinochet took power.

Not for the first time, Egypt (backed by Syria, Iraq, Morocco, Saudi Arabia, and Jordan) made a surprise attack on Israel. On 6 October, **Yom Kippur**, Egyptian troops crossed the Suez Canal while Syrians attacked the Golan Heights. Israeli troops, led by General Moshe Dayan (*left*) absorbed the attacks and then counter-attacked, pushing Syrians and Egyptians back to the 1967 ceasefire line. (*Above*) A Soviet-built Syrian Tupolev jet in action over the Golan Heights, 15 October.

track 12

The **Yom Kippur War** continued throughout October. On 16 October Israeli Premier Golda Meir rejected truce offers on the grounds that the enemy had not been "beaten enough". The Big Powers stepped in, with Kissinger flying to Moscow to meet with Soviet leaders. (*Left*) Israeli troops move up to the front line.

(*Above*) **Israeli troops** manning a French-made 155mm howitzer, shell Syrian forces on the Golan Heights, 17 October 1973. Although both West and East sought to broker a peace deal, it was Britain, France, and the Soviet Union who had supplied the arms used in the war.

(*Above*) Israeli tank crews celebrate crossing the Suez Canal into Egypt less than a month after the beginning of the war. A blindfolded **Egyptian prisoner** is perched on top of the tank. The war ended on 11 November.

Throughout 1973 students demonstrated in Athens against the **Rule of the Greek Colonels** and Prime Minister Georgius Papadopoulos (*right*). In November buses were used to barricade streets (*left*). The Army responded with force (*above*) and Papadopoulos was ousted. Martial law was then imposed.

Fascism was also under attack on the other side of Europe. On 12 June Admiral **Luis Carrero Blanco** (*left* – with General Franco on right) was appointed Prime Minister of Spain. Six months later, Blanco was killed in Madrid by a bomb planted in his car (*right*) – it blew the car 18 metres (60 feet) into the air. At a press conference on 29 December (*above*), hooded members of the Basque Separatist Movement (ETA) claimed responsibility for Blanco's death.

The superstars of Glam Rock still led the field.
(*Above*) **Rod Stewart** (centre) leads The Faces in
front of an audience of 22,000 at an open-air
concert in Los Angeles. (*Right*) **David Bowie** in
the guise of his *alter ego* Ziggy Stardust. In June
1973 he swore he would never do another gig.

Torture as entertainment or entertainment as torture? Steve McQueen (*left*) opens the door of his cell in Franklin Schaffner's **Papillon**. (*Above*) Edward Fox as the eponymous anti-hero of Fred Zinnemann's **Day of the Jackal**, described by Basil Wright as "a rare lesson in film-making in the good old manner".

O n 17 June 1972 five men, "well-dressed and wearing gloves", were arrested and charged with breaking into the headquarters of the Democratic National Committee in the Watergate complex (above), Washington DC. The leader of the group was James McCord, an ex-CIA employee. It took almost two years for the link between the bungled burglary and the White House to be clearly identified. In September 1972, the White House insisted that only the five men arrested, and two aides – Howard Hunt and Gordon Liddy – were involved. In November all seemed well for Nixon when he was re-elected as President in a landslide victory. Then, on 28 March 1973, McCord revealed that John Mitchell, former Attorney-General and head of the campaign to get Nixon re-elected, had prior knowledge of the break-in.

(*Right*) James McCord (second from left in check tie) and his attorney Bernard Fensterwald (at microphone) speak to reporters about McCord's part in the Watergate break-in, 28 March 1973. Looking on, notebook in hand, is Carl Bernstein of the *Washington Post*.

DISBURSEMENTS
KALMBACH   250,000*
STRACHAN   350,000
PORTER   100,000*
LIDDY   199,000*
MAGRUDER   20,000
LANKLER   50,000
HITT   25,000
NOFZIGER   10,000*
STONE   15,000*
DOLE   3,000
OTHER   5,000*

TOTAL   1,777,000*

*approximation

On 30 April 1973, in a televised address to the nation, Nixon accepted responsibility for Watergate, though he added that he had no prior knowledge of the affair. That same day, three White House aides and Attorney-General Richard Kleindienst resigned. (*Right*) The first four casualties of Watergate: (clockwise from top left) John W Dean III; former Attorney-General John Mitchell; John D Ehrlichman; and former White House Chief of Staff H R Bob Haldeman. (*Left*) Senator Joseph Montoya of New Mexico examines testimony at the Watergate hearings. Behind him is a chart showing donations collected by the committee to re-elect the President.

In March 1974 Nixon was named
as a co-conspirator. Impeachment
proceedings began in July. (*Left*)
Nixon hugs his daughter Julie on
the day before his resignation,
7 August 1974. (*Above*) In a world
of his own, Nixon gives a double
victory sign as he leaves the White
House following his resignation.
(*Right*) Gerald Ford (on left) is
sworn in as Nixon's successor.

By 1974 the Chancellorship of **Willy Brandt** (*left*, on left) had run its course. Although his *Ostpolitik* had been highly successful, he resigned in May 1974 when it emerged that his close associate Günter Guillaume (*left*, on right) had been working for the East German *Stasi*. (*Right*) Brandt's pragmatic and unidealogical successor **Helmut Schmidt**, former Minister of Finance.

India becomes the sixth nation to possess the Bomb. (*Right*) The crater made by the subterranean explosion of **India's first nuclear test**, 18 May 1974. The tests took place 100 metres (328 feet) underground near Pokhran in the desert state of Rajasthan. Prime Minister Indira Gandhi claimed that India's nuclear policy was peaceful, and that such explosions might be used in the mining industry.

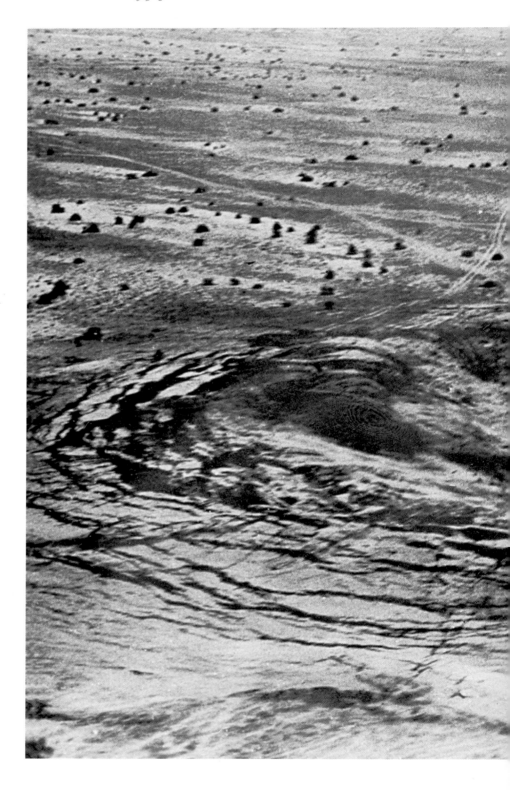

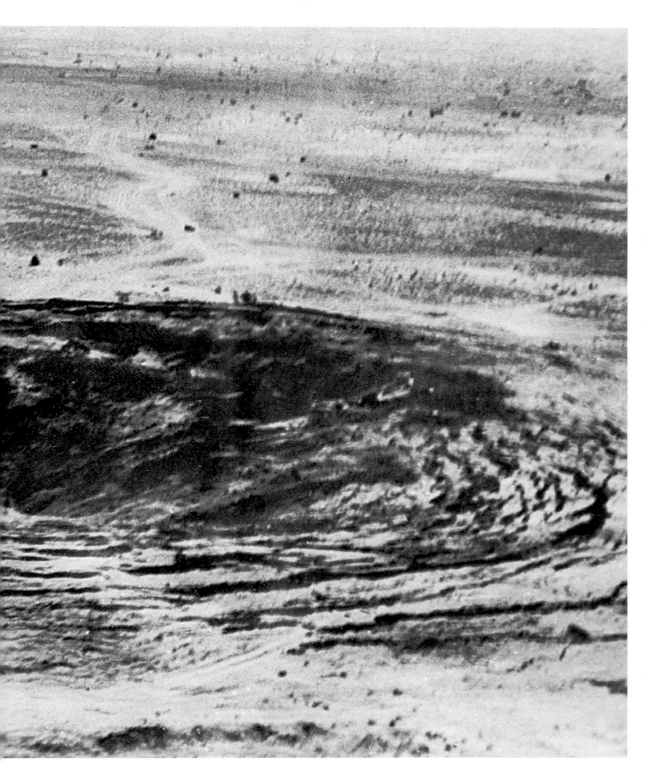

1974 saw a major **IRA bombing campaign** on mainland Britain. (*Above*) Smoke rises from Westminster Hall, London, following the detonation of a 20 lb bomb, 17 June. (*Right*) The aftermath of an explosion that killed four soldiers in the Horse and Groom, Guildford, 5 October. (*Far right*) Firemen recover some of the 23 bodies from the Tavern in the Town, Birmingham, 22 November.

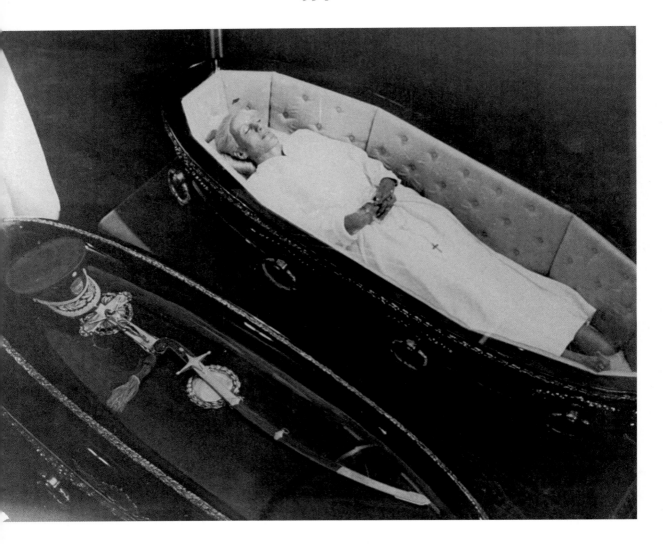

When President **Juan Perón** of Argentina died
in office in 1974 the coffin of his first wife – the
beloved Eva Perón – was flown from her tomb
in Italy and placed beside that of her husband
on public display. (*Above*) Perón's body in
open casket, Buenos Aires. In death, the
Peróns had little rest. Juan was reburied twice.

The President of France, **Georges Pompidou**, died unexpectedly of Kahler's disease – a rare condition that attacks the bone marrow – on 2 April 1974, while still in office. (*Above*) members of the French government and parliament gather in Notre Dame Cathedral for Pompidou's funeral, 8 April 1974.

The Final the whole world wanted to see...
(*Above*) And a moment that could have cost West
Germany the World Cup. Hoeness (on ground)
brings down Holland's **Johan Cruyff** (centre),
Munich, 7 July 1974. A penalty was awarded and
Johann Neeskens scored from the spot.

The West German superstar of 1974 was **Franz Beckenbauer**. Beckenbauer (*above, on right wearing "5"*) blocks a Dutch attack later in the game. Although solid in defence, Beckenbauer's great strength was his ability to launch an attack from his own half.

In the end it was a goal by Gerd Müller that
brought victory to West Germany by 2–1. (*Left*)
West German goalkeeper **Sepp Maier** holds the
new FIFA World Cup Trophy. (*Above*) Captain
Franz Beckenbauer and the West German
manager **Helmut Schön** after their team's victory.

The two outstanding tennis stars of 1974 were **Jimmy Connors** and **Chris Evert**, both of the United States. (*Above*) Connors at stretch during a match at Wimbledon, Independence Day, 1974. (*Right*) Chris Evert hurls her racket in the air after defeating the Russian Olga Morozova in the Women's Final, Wimbledon, July 1974.

Early in 1974, Archbishop Makarios (*above*) returned to **Cyprus** after years in exile, to become the country's first President. He did not hold power for long, being ousted by an army coup on 15 July. (*Left*) Nikos Sampson (second from left), leader of the coup. On 20 July, Turkish troops invaded Cyprus, but were easily repelled. (*Right*) Turkish Cypriot prisoners of war, 28 July 1974.

(*Above*) Yasser Arafat (on right) at an **Arab Summit Meeting** in Rabat, Morocco, 30 October 1974. At the meeting the PLO was recognized as "the sole legitimate representative of the Palestinian people". (*Left*) Egyptian troops celebrate President Anwar el-Sadat's decision to forge stronger links with other Arab nations.

(*Right*) Muhammad Ali punches George Foreman's image on a poster advertising **"The Rumble in the Jungle"**, Khinshasa, the Congo, October 1974. (*Above*) Foreman hits the canvas following a stinging left-and-right from Ali, who won the fight and regained the World Heavyweight Championship in the eighth round.

Hollywood proves that crime does pay with two
movie successes of 1974. (*Above*) Jack Nicholson,
restrained by Roy Jenson (right) has his nose slit by
Roman Polanski (left, back to camera) in **Chinatown**.
(*Right*) John Cazale (left) plots with Al Pacino in
Francis Ford Coppola's **The Godfather II**. Both were
nominated for Best Film Oscar. *The Godfather* won.

GF-II-5618-7

Never happy in opposition – feeling that it was somehow "unfair" – the British Tory Party changed leaders in February 1975. Out went the bumbling Heath and in came the bustling Thatcher. (*Left*) **Edward Heath** on his yacht *Morning Cloud*, May 1975. (*Right*) **Margaret Thatcher** enjoys the applause following her speech at the Conservative Party Conference, 10 October.

The Party of Democratic Kampuchea, known as the **Khmer Rouge**, had been fighting for control of Cambodia for 25 years. Backed by the Chinese they overthrew the US-backed regime of Lon Nol in the spring of 1975, capturing Phnom Penh after a three and a half month siege. (*Above and right*) Khmer Rouge soldiers enter Phnom Penh, 17 April 1975. Horror lay ahead for Cambodia.

Vietnam, 30 April 1975. In a scene reminiscent of Pearl Harbor in 1941, North Vietnamese troops sprint past burning South Vietnamese planes on the tarmac of Saigon's Tan Son Nhat airport. The airport had been bombed by the Communists at a time when fleeing refugees had swarmed over the runways, making it impossible for the planes to take off. The final collapse of South Vietnam had been swift, and the fall of the city was only a few hours away.

The last helicopter left the American Embassy in **Saigon** at 08.00 on 30 April. Four hours later a North Vietnamese tank (*above*) crashed through the gates of the Saigon presidential palace, President Duong van Minh surrendered, and it was all over. (*Right*) The moment of victory captured by Françoise de Mulder with her photograph of a North Vietnamese tank crew at the palace.

track 15

The boys were growing up, but the abstemious **Osmonds**, whose religious convictions made them shun even the mildly stimulating effect of Coca Cola, continued to be one of the top groups of the 1970s. (*Above*) Teenage fans wave their favours at an Osmonds gig in 1975. Donny Osmond was still the major heart-throb.

(*Above*) Fans of the **Bay City Rollers**, bedecked in stripes and tartan, turn out in force for a concert in Swansea, 27 May 1975. Referring to the habitual Scottish dress of the Edinburgh based group, one Teen magazine asked: "What could girls do to identify with the Osmonds? Dress up like Mormons?"

Harold Wilson's Labour government held a **referendum** on Britain's continued membership of the EEC. (*Left, top*) Margaret Thatcher, flanked by William Whitelaw (left) and Peter Kirk, was for staying. (*Left, below*) Peter Shore (on right), a member of the Labour Government was for going. (*Right*) Counting the referendum votes, 6 June 1975. The result was 2 to 1 in favour of staying in.

In July 1975 the USA and the USSR agreed on a joint space mission, the **Apollo-Soyuz Test Project**. For three days the two spacecraft were locked together in space. (*Left*) The Soviet Soyuz prepares to dock with Apollo, 16 July. (*Right*) US astronaut Thomas Stafford (on left) with Soviet cosmonaut Alexei Leonov in the hatchway of the module that joined the two spacecraft.

Not yet President of Iraq but already the most influential man in his country, **Saddam Hussein** went to southern France in 1975 to shop for weapons of limited destruction. (*Left*) Saddam Hussein arrives at the Dassault Aviation test flight centre in Istres, 8 September 1975. (*Above*) Saddam Hussein (centre) talks with French Defence Minister Yvon Bourges.

The struggle between Druze-Palestinian militia groups and Maronite Christian Phalangists turned into full scale **civil war in the Lebanon** in 1975. By December there was widespread fighting in the streets of Beirut (*above*). (*Left*) Militiamen at a barricade in the Chyal area.

So many separate sectarian, ideological, and foreign groups joined in the fighting in **Beirut** that most of the Lebanese had little understanding of what was happening. As well as the fighting between Muslims and Christians, Israeli troops began attacking Palestinians in southern Lebanon.

(*Above*) A **Katyusha rocket** is fired from the back of a truck into an apartment building in Beirut. (*Left*) One of Beirut's many narrow streets piled with rubble from the shelling, mortar and rocket attacks. The fighting was to continue for 15 years.

He used to sell insurance. By 1975 **Evel Knievel** was riding high, though sometimes not high enough. (*Right*) Knievel leaves a London hotel after failing to clear 13 single decker buses on his motorbike, 10 June. (*Above*) A triumphant return – Knievel with the 14 buses he cleared at King's Island, Ohio, 25 October.

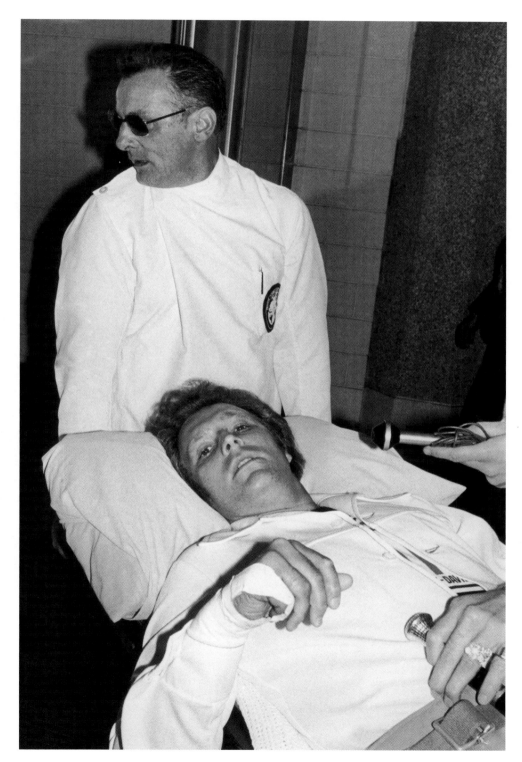

When Portugal pulled out of **Angola** in January 1975, fighting broke out between the FNLA and UNITA on one side, and the MPLA on the other. (*Left*) A banner of UNITA leader Jonas Savimbi, Independence Day, Nova Lisboa, November 1975. (*Above*) The toppled statue of the city's founder Norton de Matos.

There were those in Spain who mourned the death of **General Francisco Franco** on 20 November 1975. For the Right and the Church, Franco had been the man who saved their country from atheism and Communism in the 1930s, and who had kept an iron hand on the country ever since. For many others, his death came as liberation from a cruel past. (*Above*) Crowds read the news of his death on a Madrid street. (*Right*) Franco's body lies in state at the Pardo Palace Madrid, 24 November.

(*Above*) Right-wing leader Hanan Porat and his supporters celebrate following Israel's agreement to establish **Jewish settlements** on the West Bank, 8 December 1975. (*Left*, *top*) One of the new camps at Alon Moreh. (*Left*, *below*) Settlers at Ma'ale Edomim, between Jerusalem and the Dead Sea.

China   1976

On 8 January 1976 Zhou Enlai died of cancer. He had been China's Prime Minister since the Revolution of 1949, Mao's right hand man, and a moderating force in Chinese politics. At his funeral the eulogy was given by Deng Xiaoping, General Secretary of the Chinese Communist Party. The tone of the eulogy, praising fairness and commonsense, may well have accelerated the changes that followed.

In April Deng was ousted, following a mass protest meeting in Tiananmen Square. He fled south, to await the outcome of what seemed the inevitable power struggle. But nature intervened. A massive earthquake in the Shandong region left 300,000 Chinese dead and 500,000 wounded. Traditionally, such natural disasters were seen as portents of some matching crisis in human affairs.

The crisis came on 9 September 1976, with the death of Mao Zedong. A month later, the "Gang of Four", leaders of the Cultural Revolution of 1966, were arrested.

Following in the footsteps of Richard Nixon, and accompanied by Deng Xiaoping, US President Gerald Ford reviews Chinese troops, December 1975.

Heroes and villains. (*Above*) Demonstrators pay homage to the memory of Zhou Enlai. (*Right*) Protestors denounce Vice President Deng Xiaoping. Both events took place in Tiananmen Square, April 1976.

Members of the Chinese Popular
Army hurry to play their part in
clearing the devastation caused by
the Shandong earthquake, 11 August
1976. China refused all foreign aid.

(*Above*) Mourning Chinese file past the body of Mao Zedong, lying in state in Beijing, 12 September 1976. To preserve the body in the hot weather, doctors had injected the corpse with 22 litres of formaldehyde. As a result, Mao's own physician reported that "the face was bloated... neck now the width of his head... ears sticking out at right angles..."

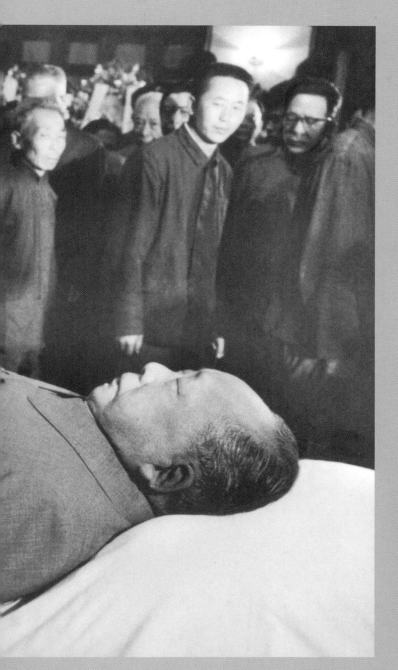

(*Above*) Mao's widow, Chiang Ch'ing, once the most powerful woman in China, at the time of her arrest, October 1976. (*Below*) Hua Guofeng, Chairman of the Communist Party and scourge of the Gang of Four, November 1976.

The fighting in the **Lebanon** began in April 1975, when unidentified gunmen fired on a Christian church in East Beirut. Maronite Phalangists retaliated by killing 27 Palestinians. In July Israeli troops entered South Lebanon. Two months later the Syrian army invaded North Lebanon. By early 1976 a full scale war was in progress throughout the country. (*Right*) Christian forces invade Karantina, a slum district populated by poor Kurds and Armenians, but allegedly controlled by PLO detachments, 19 January 1976. More than 1,000 civilians were massacred.

With the departure of Portuguese troops in late 1975, civil war broke out in **Angola** between pro-Western forces (UNITA, FLNA) and the Marxist MPLA. (*Left*) Child soldiers of the MPLA on a military parade, 16 February 1976. (*Above*) A young warrior takes a rest beneath a portrait of MPLA leader Agostinho Neto, 23 February 1976.

In the summer of 1976, the South African government
ordered that the Afrikaans language was to be taught in
all schools. In the **Soweto** suburb of Johannesburg,
10,000 African students protested, seeing Afrikaans as
a symbol of white domination. Police opened fire, killing
100 protesters. (*Above*) Rioters use cars as road blocks.
(*Right*) The face of desperation, Soweto, 21 June 1976.

(*Left*) **Björn Borg** celebrates the
first of his five successive
Wimbledon Championships after
defeating Ilya Nastase, 3 July 1976.
(*Above*) The darling of the
Seventies tennis fans, **Chris Evert**
on her way to winning the Women's
title in the same tournament.

At 07.53 EST, 19 June 1976, the **US Viking 1 Lander** separated from its spacecraft and landed at Chryse Planitia on the surface of Mars. It had taken 11 months from launch to get there. *Viking 1*'s mission was to obtain high resolution images of the planet. (*Right*) The surface of Mars, one of the first colour images to be transmitted to earth from another planet.

The USSR and East German teams dominated the 1976 Montreal Olympic Games, winning 215 medals between them. The Games were a personal triumph for swimmer **Kornelia Ender** (*left*) of the GDR, who won four gold and two silver medals. But, for many, the star of the Games was the diminutive 14-year-old **Nadia Comaneci** (*right*) of Romania, who won three golds in the Women's Gymnastic events.

At the Montreal Olympics, **Alberto Juantorena** of Cuba became the first man to take gold in both the 400 Metres and 800 Metres since Paul Pilgrim in the Intercalated Games at Athens in 1906. (*Left*) Juantorena takes the lead in the final of the Men's 800 Metres.

Another double gold winner at Montreal was **Lasse Viren** of Finland, who won both the Men's 5,000 Metres and 10,000 Metres event. (*Above*) Viren wins the 5,000 Metres, with Dick Quax (691) taking silver, and Klaus-Peter Hildenbrand diving for bronze.

The **Notting Hill Riots** in West London brought the 1976
Carnival to a sad and savage end. Trouble started on the
afternoon of 30 August when police attempted to arrest
a suspected pickpocket. Violence erupted. Gangs of
white and black youths rioted and attacked the police.
(*Right*) Police head for safety – 100 of them were injured.
(*Above*) A street littered with debris following the rioting.

After two successive Presidential election defeats, the Democrats were back in business following **Jimmy Carter**'s victory in November 1976. (*Above*) Carter on the stump in New York City, October 1976. (*Right*) Carter and his wife Rosalynn enjoy a celebratory hug after news of the Democrats narrow victory over Gerald Ford comes in, 2 November 1976.

The Uses and Abuses of Art, 1976.
(*Left*) **Alexander Calder** paints his prototype design for the Braniff International Boeing fleet. (*Above*) **Tom Keating** stands in front of his fake *Hay Wain*, in the style of John Constable, August 1976.

Two box office film successes of 1976.
(*Left*) Sylvester Stallone in a still
from the Oscar winning **Rocky**.
(*Above*) Harvey Stephens, as Damien,
in a promotional still for **The Omen**.

The "glam" of Glam Rock was freely construed. (*Left*) The American band **Kiss** on Westminster Bridge, London during their first European tour: (left to right) Paul Stanley, Peter Criss, Ace Frehley, and Gene Simmons. (*Above*) **David Bowie** relaxes with Romy Haag after performing at the Pavilion, Paris, 18 May 1976.

(*Above*) The first date of the "Anarchy Tour", The Damned at Leeds Polytechnic, 6 December 1976 – (left to right) Brian James (bass), Dave Vanian (vocals), and Rat Scabies (drums). (*Left*) Malcolm McLaren, co-owner of the SEX boutique and manager of The Sex Pistols.

Here was a movement that fused music and fashion in the heat of anger and attitude. Punks had no wish to look or sound beautiful. The names of the bands and the artists revealed the toughness of the approach – The Clash, The Damned, Johnny Rotten (*left*), and Sid Vicious. Punk's founding figures were often alienated, surly kids whose rage produced a great new sound.

The fashion that followed the music – with dog collars and safety pins. (*Far left*) Fans of The Sex Pistols in graffiti daubed T shirts, July 1977. Two more punk rockers: (*above*) Karen from Sweden, decorated with back to front swastika, and (*left*) a rocker at the Rainbow, with NO FUTURE on her forehead.

(*Above*) Punk rock fans tear up the seats at a gig by The Jam and The Clash, Rainbow Theatre, London, 14 May 1977. (*Left*) Paul Simonon of The Clash at the same gig. (*Right*) Debbie Harry, lead singer with the American band Blondie, May 1977.

As part of the 1977 celebrations for her **Silver Jubilee**, Queen Elizabeth II spent February and March touring the Commonwealth. On her return to Britain, she faced further tours of the United Kingdom, church services, addresses of loyalty from both Houses of Parliament, bonfires, functions, a Royal Progress down the Thames, and the Sex Pistols' own version of *God Save the Queen*. (*Above*, left to right) Princess Anne, Earl Mountbatten, Her Majesty, and the Duke of Edinburgh on the balcony of Buckingham Palace, 28 June 1977. (*Right*) A loyal London home, 3 June 1977.

There was plenty to fight about on the home front. (*Left*) **Gays**, and others, march along King's Road, Chelsea in protest at the conviction of *Gay News* for blasphemous libel, 30 July 1977. (*Above*) One of the victims of the Battle of Lewisham, 12 August 1977. Some 5,000 **anti-Fascists** prevented a National Front March through south-east London.

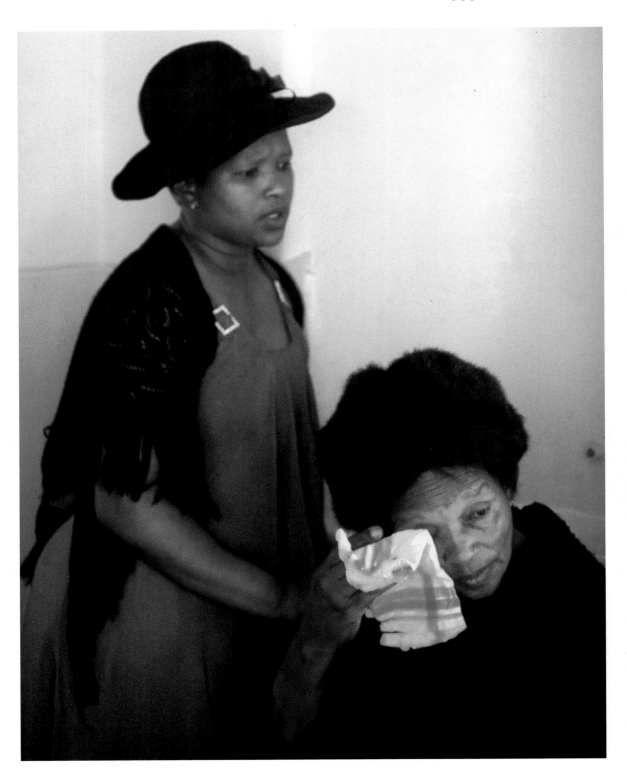

"The greatest man I have ever had the privilege to know" – Donald Woods. (*Above*) **Steve Biko**'s coffin is carried to the cemetery at King William's Town, South Africa, 5 September 1977. Biko, founder of the SA Black Consciousness Movement, was beaten to death while in police custody. (*Left*) A portrait of Steve Biko, carried at his funeral. (*Far left*) Biko's wife Ntsikie (left) and mother Alice at Biko's inquest.

197

(*Left*) **Jean-Bédel Bokassa**, self-proclaimed Emperor of the Central African Republic, at his extravagant coronation, Bangui, 4 December 1977. The event cost $20 million, a quarter of the country's GNP. (*Above*) **Haile Mariam Mengistu**, new leader of Ethiopia after successfully ousting Haile Selassie, May 1977. Bokassa was overthrown ten years later. Mengistu survived civil war and became President when Ethiopia reverted to civilian rule.

(*Above*) Three of **The Rolling Stones** (left to right – Mick Jagger, Ronnie Wood, and Keith Richards) celebrate the release of their *Love You Live* album at Trax nightclub, New York, 23 September 1977. (*Right*) Freddie Mercury at a **Queen** sell-out concert, Earl's Court, London, 11 June 1977.

John Travolta, as Tony Manero, contemplates the complexities of love in a New York subway car on the set of John Badham's **Saturday Night Fever**. The critics were unimpressed, but the film grossed almost $100 million at the box office and gained Travolta an Oscar nomination.

Another angle on the Big Apple... (*Above*)
Woody Allen (right, with Diane Keaton) also
won an Oscar nomination for Best Actor in
his **Annie Hall**. Critics loved the film, it took
four Oscars, and was also a commercial
success for Allen, grossing $40 million.

The film was intended for a generation growing up without fairy tales. The happy ending and the pot of gold went to director George Lucas (right), and his wife and editor Marcia Lucas, seen here in a Los Angeles edit suite working on **Star Wars**.

(*Above*) On the largest film set then used in movie history – an old dirigible hangar – Steven Spielberg directs a scene from **Close Encounters of the Third Kind**. The film cost $20 million to make, but Spielberg got his money back and an Oscar nomination for Best Director.

Jan-Carl RASPE
Arrested: Frankfurt, 1 June 1972
Suicide: Stammheim, 18 October 1977

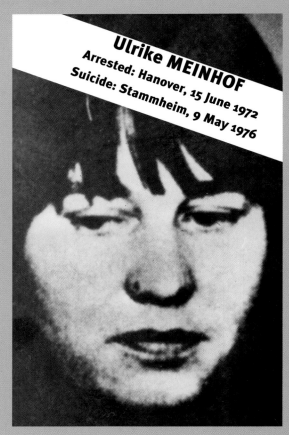

Ulrike MEINHOF
Arrested: Hanover, 15 June 1972
Suicide: Stammheim, 9 May 1976

Gudrun ENSSLIN
Arrested: Hamburg, 7 June 1972
Suicide: Stammheim, 18 October 1977

(*Above and right*) Some of the leaders of the Red Army Faction. In prison, they were kept in solitary confinement, denied visitors, and force fed when they went on hunger strike. (*Far right*) The arrest of Andreas Baader by Frankfurt police, June 1972.

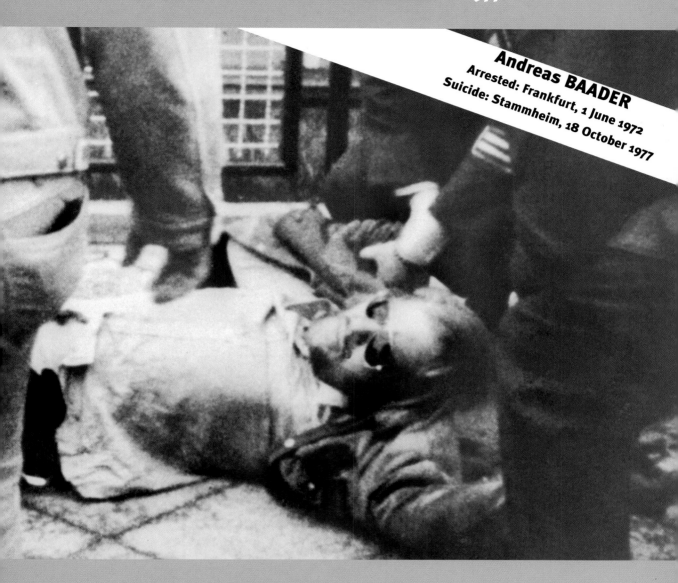

Andreas BAADER
Arrested: Frankfurt, 1 June 1972
Suicide: Stammheim, 18 October 1977

The two most active and feared terrorist organizations in Europe in the Seventies were the Red Army Faction or RAF (better known as the Baader-Meinhof gang), and the Red Brigades. The RAF operated primarily in Germany where they aimed to expose by violent means what they saw as the lurking Fascism of the new consumer society. Their targets were bankers and industrialists as well as politicians. The Red Brigades were centred in Italy, where they carried out 14,000 terrorist attacks in the 1970s alone. Both groups survived into the 1990s, but the RAF virtually ceased to exist with the collapse of Communist East Germany, their main backers.

RAF members suspected
of killing (*above*) the
industrialist Hans-Martin
Schleyer (*right*): (*clockwise
from top left*) Christian
Klar, Elisabeth Von Dyck,
Brigitte Mohnhaupt,
Silke Maier-Witt, Jörg Lang,
Friederike Krabbe, Rolf
Heissler, and Rolf Wagner.

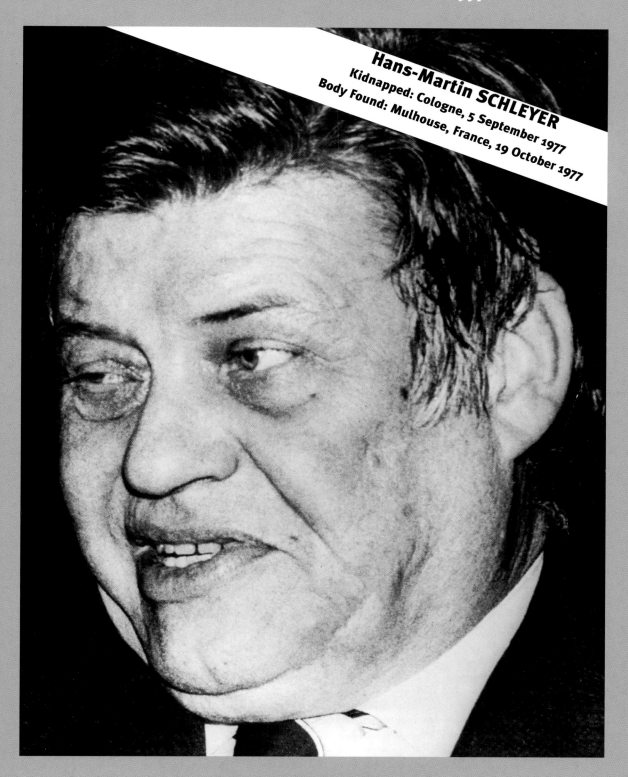

Hans-Martin SCHLEYER
Kidnapped: Cologne, 5 September 1977
Body Found: Mulhouse, France, 19 October 1977

In 1978 the Red Brigades kidnapped the Italian former Prime Minister, Aldo Moro (*far right*). After holding him for 54 days, they killed him, leaving his body in the back of a van (*above*), 9 May 1978. (*Right*) Renato Curcio, leader of the Red Brigades stands trial behind bars in Turin for Moro's murder.

Aldo MORO
Kidnapped: Rome, 16 March 1978
Body Found: Rome, 9 May 1978

The civil war in **Lebanon** intensified. 3,000 Israeli troops invaded the south after a terrorist attack on a bus near Tel Aviv killed 30 Israelis. UN troops were sent in to restore order, but the chaos and the carnage continued. Two images by French photographer Françoise de Mulder: (*left*) A fighter in Tyre during the Israeli invasion, March 1978; (*above*) The blazing refinery at Gilded, Beirut.

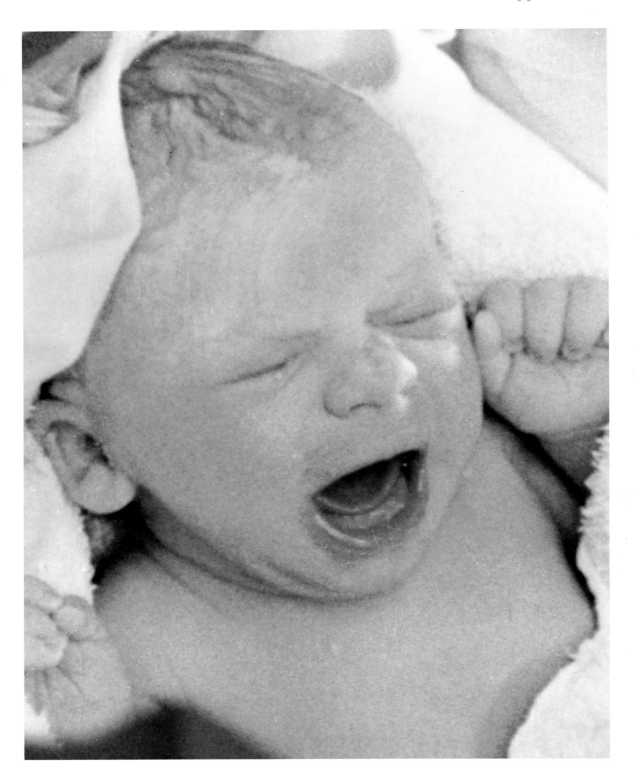

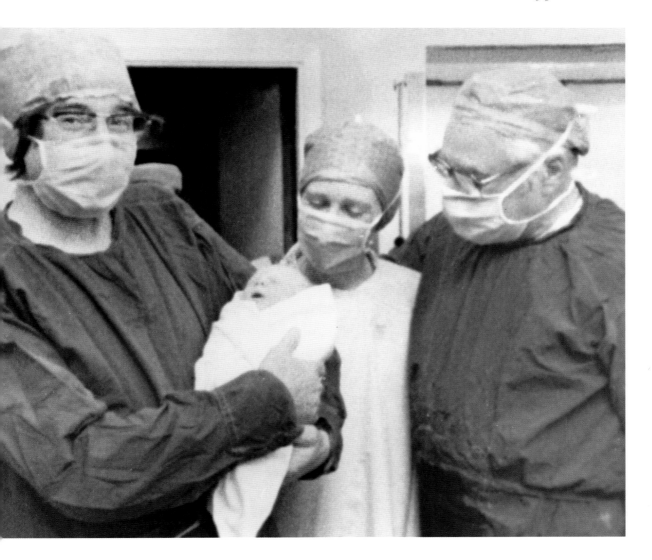

Louise Joy Brown, the **world's first test-tube baby** (*left*) was born at the Oldham General Hospital, Lancashire on 25 July 1978. (*Above*) The team at the Hospital: (left, holding Louise) physiologist Robert Edwards and (right) Patrick Steptoe, the gynaecologist who pioneered in-vitro fertilization. It took 12 years to perfect the method of conception outside the human body.

It took President Carter 13 days of determined
shuttle diplomacy between Egyptian and Israeli
delegations to clinch two remarkable deals
at the **Camp David Summit**. Both deals laid the
groundwork for closer co-operation and better
relations between the two countries.

(*Left*) The men who made the deals: (left to right) Prime Minister Menachem Begin of Israel, Carter and President Anwar El-Sadat of Egypt. (*Above*) Former enemies embrace in the East Room of the White House after signing the **Peace Agreement**, 18 September 1978.

🔘 **track 20**

Party people gather in New York. (*Above*, left to right) *Interview* magazine editor Bob Colacello, Jerry Hall, Andy Warhol, Debbie Harry (with magazine cover picture behind her), Truman Capote, and Paloma Picasso at **Studio 54**. (*Left*) Yves St Laurent and Nan Kempner celebrate the launch of "Opium" perfume at the South Street Seaport Museum.

(*Above*) **Sid Vicious**, bass player with the Sex Pistols, on stage with American singer and girl-friend **Nancy Spungen**. Sharing a growing heroin addiction, they were an inseparable couple until 13 October 1978, when Spungen was found dead in New York's Chelsea Hotel. Sid was arrested (*right*) and charged with her murder. He overdosed and died while on bail.

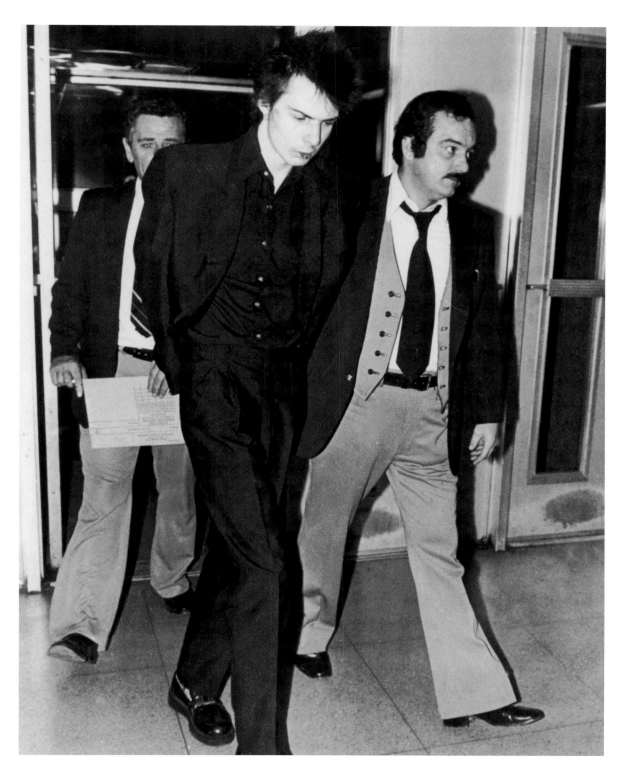

A month later, Pope John Paul I died of a heart attack. Cardinal Wojtyla, the first non-Italian pope for four centuries, succeeded him as **Pope John Paul II**. (*Right*) The new Pope makes his first public appearance following his election, 16 October 1978.

Following the death of Pope Paul VI and one of the swiftest papal elections of modern times, Albino Luciani, Patriarch of Venice, became **Pope John Paul I** on 26 August 1978. (*Above*) John Paul I (on left) is congratulated by Polish Cardinal Karol Wojtyla.

As in all revolutions, two forces worked to overthrow the Shah's regime in Iran. The push came from mounting hatred of the country's security organization Savak, seen by the poor as a vicious weapon of repression, and by widespread poverty. The pull came from a widespread belief that Iran's redemption lay in turning to the mullahs, and in particular to the exiled Ayatollah Ruhollah Khomeini (opposite). For some time taped messages from the Ayatollah had been smuggled into Iran. The crisis came to a head when a wave of strikes in major industries brought the country to a standstill late in 1978.

(*Above*) **The Ayatollah Khomeini greets a visitor to the garden of his French home at Neauphle le Château on the outskirts of Paris, 8 November 1978. It was the final stop on an exile that had lasted 15 years.**

Comings and goings at Mehrabad Airport, Tehran. (*Above*) Mohammad Reza Pahlavi, Shah of Iran, shakes hands with Prime Minister Shapour Baktiar 10 days before finally leaving Iran. (*Left*) The Shah goes into exile, 16 January 1979. (*Right*) Ayatollah Khomeini leaves his Air France Boeing 747 flight from Paris, 1 February 1979.

(*Above*) A few days after the Shah's departure, members of the Iranian Islamic Army show their solidarity with civilian demonstrators calling for the return of the Ayatollah. (*Left*) The day after his arrival in Tehran, Ayatollah Khomeini receives the adulation of his supporters. Prime Minister Baktiar had insisted the secular government would stand firm against Islamic rule. Within days he had lost power.

In January 1979, **Pol Pot** was finally ousted from Cambodia after the Khmer Rouge's four-year reign of terror had resulted in the deaths of more than one million people. Pol Pot and his principal henchman Feng Sari were sentenced to death in their absence. (*Above*) A paint-daubed bust of Pol Pot. (*Right*) Racks of skulls and bones of slaughtered Cambodians, evidence of Pol Pot's barbarism.

UNNECESSARY PERSONNEL
STAY BEHIND LINES

In March 1979 a combination of equipment failure and human error led to the threat of meltdown at the US nuclear plant at **Three Mile Island**, Pennsylvania (*right*). (opposite) A Civil Defense volunteer checks radiation levels at the plant, 2 April 1979. (*Above*) President Jimmy Carter (centre) and his wife pay a visit to the crippled site.

On 30 April 1978 the Afghan Khalq Communist Party staged a coup, removing and assassinating the President of the Republic, Daoud Khan. The new regime was immediately recognized by the Soviet Union, who sent in troops (*above*) to support the Communist government. In December 1978, Moscow signed a 20 year friendship pact with **Afghanistan**. Two months later, US Ambassador Adolph Dubs was murdered. (*Right*) Young Communist supporters mark the first anniversary of the Communist coup, Kabul, 28 April 1979.

(*Above*) Kneeling in reverence, **Margaret Thatcher**, leader of the Conservative Party plays the devoted disciple of ex-Prime Minister Harold Macmillan during his 85th birthday party at the Carlton Club, London, 7 February 1979. The reverence did not last long. In May she became Prime Minister and embarked on a series of policies that shook old Toryism to the core. (*Right*) Margaret and Denis Thatcher acknowledge the cheers of their followers outside 10 Downing Street, 5 May 1979.

In 1976 **Jeremy Thorpe** resigned as leader of the British Liberal party
following allegations of a homosexual relationship with **Norman Scott**
(*left*). Three years later, Thorpe was charged with conspiracy and incitement
to murder Scott. (*Above*) Thorpe arrives at the Old Bailey in London for his
trial, 18 June 1979. Thorpe was acquitted, but his career was ruined.

(*Left*) **Fidel Castro** addresses the United Nations General Assembly, 12 October 1979. His four and a half hour speech was a statement of the will of 95 non-aligned countries that international relations no longer be based on "injustice, inequality, and oppression". (*Above*) US Secretary of State Cyrus Vance (on left) applauds as Jimmy Carter and Leonid Brezhnev shake hands at the **SALT II** negotiations in Vienna, 19 June 1979.

The Red threat drew nearer to the United States in 1979 when the 46 year long rule of the Somoza family in **Nicaragua** came to an abrupt end. General Anastasia Somoza fled the country, and the Sandinistas took over. They embarked on a series of socialist measures that included nationalization of key industries, the restoration of human rights, and an end to capital punishment. (*Right*) Interior Minister Thomas Borge (centre, left arm raised) acknowledges the crowd in the Plaza de la Revolucion, Managua, 20 July 1979.

Targets of Irish extremism. (*Left*) Wreckage of a car bombed by the Irish National Liberation Army in which the Conservative Party Northern Ireland spokesman, **Airey Neave**, was killed at Westminster, 31 March 1979. (*Right*) The funeral of **Lord Louis Mountbatten**, 5 September 1979. Mountbatten was murdered by a bomb while sailing near his home in County Sligo, Ireland.

Two weeks after the return of Ayatollah Khomeini, the US Embassy in Tehran was attacked. Two Marines were injured. It was a taste of what was to come. On 4 November a hostile crowd seized the Embassy, taking 100 staff and Marines hostage. (*Above*) Blindfolded **US hostages** are paraded at the Embassy, 8 November. (*Right*) A young protester at yet another demonstration, 29 November. After a botched rescue attempt in April, the hostages were freed in May 1980.

Rhodesia held elections in April 1979. Although Prime Minister Ian Smith (*right*) was ousted, the new constitution he had piloted through parliament resulted in victory for the moderate UANC and Abel Muzorewa – ZANU and ZAPU, the extreme black parties had declined to take part. The Bush War continued. (*Above*) A white Rhodesian woman practices firing a sub-machine gun, 22 May 1979.

The move towards full independence for the newly named
Zimbabwe continued. (*Right*) Founder and leader of ZANU
Robert Mugabe arrives at Lancaster House, London for
the Zimbabwe Rhodesia Constitutional Conference,
10 September 1979. (*Above*) Three months later, Abel
Muzorewa (left) and Lord Carrington, British Foreign
Secretary, sign the **Lancaster House Agreement**, 21
December 1979. A ceasefire was agreed. Independence
soon followed, but the misery was to return.

(*Right*) The designer, the model and the bolts of fabric are real – the statues and the ornate carvings are painted illusions. Newly independent but already internationally famous fashion leader **Giorgio Armani** poses in Milan, May 1979. (*Left*) A black velvet jacket and taffeta trellis print dress by **Marc Bohan** for the House of Dior.

(*Left*) The German artist, environmentalist and anti-nuclear campaigner **Joseph Beuys** at work in the Guggenheim Museum, New York City, November 1979. Beuys believed that all creativity was essentially a therapeutic process. (*Right*) The Bulgarian born US *avant garde* sculptor **Christo Javacheff**, April 1979. It was not a good year for Christo, who failed to realize his Mastaba project, a plan to stack oil barrels 150-metres (490-feet) high.

Index
Page numbers refer to text references